SHAKESPEARE'S GREEN IMAGINATION

DR A J MANJU

MS M LINJU

Contents

Authors

Dr. A. J. Manju is an Associate Professor and Head of the Department of English at Sree Narayana Guru College, Coimbatore, with 27 years of experience in higher education. Over the course of her distinguished career, she has successfully guided 20 M.Phil. and 4 Ph.D. scholars. Her primary area of research interest lies in Afro-American literature, with a focus on themes of identity, resistance, and cultural expression. A committed educator and researcher, Dr. Manju continues to contribute significantly to literary scholarship and academic mentorship.

Ms. Linju M is an Assistant Professor of English at Nehru Arts and Science College, Coimbatore, with three years of teaching experience. She is currently pursuing her Ph.D. in English Literature, focusing on Ecoliterature and Indian Literature. Her academic interests lie in exploring environmental themes within literary and cultural contexts, and she actively contributes to the discourse on ecological awareness through literary scholarship.

Acknowledgements

I extend my sincere gratitude to Sree Narayana Guru College, Coimbatore, for fostering a vibrant academic atmosphere that continually inspires scholarly inquiry. My heartfelt thanks to my colleagues in the Department of English for their constant encouragement and critical insights throughout the development of this work.

I am especially grateful to my research scholars and students, whose inquisitive engagement with Shakespearean texts and ecological thought gave fresh impetus to my reflections. Their questions often led me to deeper explorations.

Special thanks to the library staff and all those who helped me access essential resources, and to the many scholars whose work on ecocriticism and early modern literature informed my thinking.

Above all, I thank my family for their enduring support, patience, and belief in my intellectual pursuits.

— Dr. A. J. Manju

Prologue

"One touch of nature makes the whole world kin."
— Troilus and Cressida, Act III, Scene 3

Shakespeare's works echo with the rhythms of nature—forests, tempests, seasons, and gardens—all alive with meaning. This book explores how his plays and poems reflect an ecological imagination far ahead of his time. In rereading Shakespeare through a green lens, we uncover not only his reverence for the natural world, but also a subtle awareness of its fragility.

In an era facing environmental crisis, Shakespeare's Green Imagination invites readers to listen anew to the Bard's voice—one that speaks as much to the earth as to the human spirit.

— Dr. A. J. Manju
Ms M Linju

CHAPTER ONE

ECOLOGY, ENCHANTMENT, AND THE ELIZABETHAN WORLDVIEW

William Shakespeare's works, though written centuries before the rise of modern environmentalism, pulse with ecological insight and reverence for the natural world. To understand Shakespeare's "green imagination," one must consider the ecological sensibilities embedded in the Elizabethan worldview—a perspective shaped by enchantment, hierarchy, and deep interconnectedness between the human and nonhuman realms.

The Enchanted World of Nature

The Elizabethan cosmos was not a mechanistic system, but a living, enchanted world animated by spirit, symbolism, and moral consequence. Nature was not mere backdrop but a dynamic force—capricious, moral, and sometimes punitive. In plays like A Midsummer Night's Dream, the disruption of natural harmony caused by Oberon and Titania's quarrel results in climatic chaos:

"The spring, the summer,
The childing autumn, angry winter, change
Their wonted liveries, and the mazed world,
By their increase, now knows not which is which."

Shakespeare dramatizes ecological imbalance as a consequence of moral and relational disorder. The seasons themselves become characters in a drama of cosmic consequence—proof of a worldview where ecology is deeply entangled with ethics and enchantment.

Nature as Moral Agent

Shakespeare's green imagination frequently casts nature as a moral and political agent. In King Lear, the storm on the heath is more than weather; it externalizes Lear's inner turmoil and the fractured bonds of kingship and kinship. The wild landscape becomes a stage where human pride confronts elemental power. The ecological imagery reflects the breakdown of the "Great Chain of Being," an Elizabethan concept that linked all forms of life in a divinely ordained hierarchy.

Even in The Tempest, nature is not just scenery but a site of contested power. Prospero's manipulation of natural forces through magic reflects Renaissance anxieties about control over nature, colonial authority, and the loss of harmony with the nonhuman world.

The Forest and the Wild as Liminal Spaces

Forests in Shakespeare often serve as sites of transformation, freedom, and ecological diversity. In As You Like It, the Forest of Arden is both a real and symbolic refuge from courtly corruption. It is a space of pastoral simplicity, where characters reflect, reconcile, and realign themselves with deeper truths.

The forest acts as a green counterworld—one that resists linear power structures and invites a slower, more contemplative rhythm. In these wild spaces, Shakespeare allows nature to speak not only as setting but as co-creator of change.

Pre-ecological Thinking in the Bard's Time

Though the term "ecology" had not yet been coined, Shakespeare's writing reflects pre-ecological thought—an awareness of the interdependence between species, climates, and cosmic forces. Elizabethan England was undergoing environmental shifts: deforestation, changing agricultural practices, and proto-industrial pressures. Shakespeare's works offer subtle critiques and portrayals of these changes—not as didactic warnings, but as deeply felt reckonings with the vulnerability of both nature and human society.

Conclusion: Toward a Shakespearean Environmental Ethics

Revisiting Shakespeare through an ecological lens does not anachronistically impose modern concerns onto early modern texts. Rather, it reveals the enduring capacity of literature to engage with the natural world in ways that are morally rich, emotionally potent, and philosophically profound. Shakespeare's enchanted ecology offers a compelling counterpoint to today's disenchantment—reminding us that to imagine a sustainable future, we may need to recover older, more relational ways of seeing nature.

CHAPTER TWO

NATURE, POWER, AND THE POETICS OF THE ENVIRONMENT

In the works of William Shakespeare, nature is never just a backdrop. It is a living, breathing force—sometimes beautiful, sometimes violent, often deeply political. As the environmental humanities increasingly turn to literature for deeper insights into the relationship between human societies and the natural world, Shakespeare's plays stand out for their potent blend of ecological imagery, political symbolism, and poetic depth. The Bard's vision of nature is inseparable from his exploration of power and language; it is through poetic engagement that environmental meaning emerges, charged with ethical and political resonance.

Nature as a Political Mirror

Nature in Shakespeare is frequently a mirror for the workings of power and the fragility of human order. In Macbeth, the disruption of natural order reflects the unnatural act of regicide. Following Duncan's murder, the skies darken, falcons are killed by owls, and Duncan's horses turn wild and cannibalistic:

"A falcon, towering in her pride of place,
Was by a mousing owl hawk'd at and kill'd."
(Macbeth, 2.4)

This inversion of natural hierarchy parallels Macbeth's violent usurpation of the throne. Here, nature acts as a responsive field—an ecological register of moral and political transgression. The poetics of Shakespeare's language intensify the effect, rendering the environment not as passive but as dramatically animated by human acts.

Storms, Sovereignty, and the Environment

Weather phenomena in Shakespeare are often loaded with symbolic weight. In King Lear, the storm on the heath is both literal and metaphorical. As Lear rages against the elements, stripped of power and identity, the natural world becomes a stage for existential and political collapse:

"Blow, winds, and crack your cheeks! Rage! Blow!"

The storm is not merely meteorological; it echoes the breakdown of authority and the failure of the state. Shakespeare's poetic treatment of the storm invites us to consider how environmental forces intersect with human vulnerability, governance, and emotional extremity.

In The Tempest, the titular storm is deliberately conjured by Prospero. This manipulation of nature through magic allegorizes colonial domination and raises ethical questions about control over both land and life. Caliban, described as "a thing of darkness," is closely tied to the island's ecology and represents a voice of the colonized, one who resents the violent intrusion upon the natural world he calls home.

The Pastoral and the Poetic Idealization of Nature

While nature often signifies disruption in the tragedies, it can offer renewal and simplicity in the comedies and romances. As You Like It transports its characters to the Forest of Arden—a space of refuge, transformation, and philosophical reflection. Shakespeare's pastoral mode idealizes the environment as an antidote to the corruption of court life:

"And this our life, exempt from public haunt,
Finds tongues in trees, books in the running brooks,
Sermons in stones, and good in everything."

This poetic rendering of the environment suggests a sacred literacy of the land, where nature itself is full of meaning and moral guidance. But even in these idealized settings, Shakespeare complicates the bucolic vision. The forest is also a place of uncertainty, labor, and negotiation. His nature is not Edenic; it is poetic, dynamic, and ethically charged.

Ecology and Language: Poetics as Environmental Consciousness

Shakespeare's use of metaphor, personification, and imagery is not just aesthetic—it is ecological. His poetics call attention to the permeability between human and nonhuman realms. In many plays, flora and fauna are embedded in metaphors of politics, desire, death, and rebirth. This constant entanglement suggests an early awareness of the interdependence of all life systems.

For example, in Hamlet, the decay of Denmark is imagined through ecological metaphors:

"Something is rotten in the state of Denmark."

The rot is political, but it also suggests environmental degradation—a poisoned world infected by betrayal and corruption.

Conclusion: Power, Poetry, and Planetary Thought

To read Shakespeare today is to engage with a poetics of the environment that remains startlingly relevant. His works foreground the tensions between human ambition and natural order, between sovereignty and stewardship. Nature in Shakespeare is never neutral—it is political, moral, and always mediated through the poetic. As we face global ecological crises, Shakespeare's environmental imagination invites us to reflect on how power structures impact the planet and how language itself might help us reimagine our relationship with the Earth.

CHAPTER THREE

REIMAGINING THE NATURAL WORLD IN THE BARD'S WORKS

Reimagining the Natural World in the Bard's Works

William Shakespeare's engagement with the natural world goes far beyond poetic embellishment. Across his dramatic and poetic corpus, nature is not merely observed—it is reimagined. The Bard's works invite readers and audiences to see nature as a participant in human drama, a mirror to political and psychological landscapes, and, at times, a force entirely beyond human comprehension or control. This reimagining reveals a vision of nature that is dynamic, morally complex, and deeply intertwined with the human condition.

The Living Landscape: Nature as Character

One of the most striking ways Shakespeare reimagines nature is by personifying it—not only describing natural forces, but giving them agency. Storms, forests, animals, and even seasons become characters in their own right, participating in the unfolding drama. In King Lear, the tempest on the heath is more than weather; it is the outer expression of Lear's internal disintegration and the broader collapse of natural and political order. The storm is not incidental—it is co-author of the tragedy:

"I am a man more sinned against than sinning."
(King Lear, 3.2)

Nature here functions as both witness and judge, its violence echoing the moral disorder caused by human actions. Shakespeare thus reimagines the natural world as a morally reactive system—attuned to the imbalance wrought by betrayal, ambition, and pride.

The Forest as Site of Renewal and Disruption

In Shakespeare's comedies and romances, the natural world is often represented through the forest—an ambiguous space of both liberation and testing. The Forest of Arden in As You Like It is a prime example. Removed from the rigid hierarchies of the court, the forest becomes a place where social roles are suspended, identities are remade, and wisdom is gleaned through dialogue with the land:

"Under the greenwood tree,
Who loves to lie with me,
And turn his merry note
Unto the sweet bird's throat..."

The forest reimagines society, not by rejecting civilization entirely, but by proposing a more naturalized, egalitarian mode of life rooted in observation and self-reflection. At the same time, Shakespeare resists reducing nature to an idealized, pastoral dream. The forest can also be a site of confusion, hunger, and struggle—a space where the wildness of the human mind is mirrored in the landscape.

Nature and the Supernatural: Between Science and Enchantment

The natural world in Shakespeare often borders the supernatural. In A Midsummer Night's Dream, the woods outside Athens are home to fairies, potions, and magical transformations. Nature is infused with enchantment—a realm where the boundaries between species, identities, and realities blur:

"I know a bank where the wild thyme blows,
Where oxlips and the nodding violet grows..."

Through such imagery, Shakespeare invites us to view nature not through a rationalist or mechanistic lens, but as a living matrix of possibility and transformation. This enchanted view of nature challenges the emerging scientific worldview of his time, suggesting that mystery and meaning still reside in the natural world.

Rewriting the Human-Nature Relationship

Perhaps most importantly, Shakespeare's reimagining of nature involves rethinking the place of the human within it. In The Tempest, the island setting becomes a space where power, colonization, and the environment intersect. Prospero's control of the island's elements through magic speaks to human ambition to master nature—yet this mastery is shown to be flawed and ethically troubling. Caliban, often interpreted as a symbol of the colonized subject, has a visceral connection to the land:

"This island's mine, by Sycorax my mother,
Which thou tak'st from me..."

Shakespeare anticipates modern ecological critiques of domination and control by dramatizing the tensions between knowledge, exploitation, and ecological belonging.

Conclusion: The Bard's Ecological Vision

Shakespeare's reimagining of the natural world resists simple binaries: nature is neither wholly benevolent nor merely chaotic. Instead, it is relational, responsive, and richly textured. Whether it appears as tempest or refuge, enchantment or wilderness, nature in the Bard's works is always in conversation with the human spirit.

In an age grappling with environmental degradation and climate uncertainty, returning to Shakespeare can reawaken our awareness of the Earth's moral and imaginative power. His works offer a profound literary ecology—one that challenges us not only to appreciate nature's beauty, but to question our place within its ever-shifting rhythms.

CHAPTER FOUR

ENVIRONMENTAL THOUGHT IN THE PLAYS AND POEMS OF SHAKESPEARE

Though the word environment did not enter the English language until centuries after William Shakespeare's death, his works are imbued with a sensitivity to the natural world that closely aligns with contemporary ecological thought. In both his plays and poems, Shakespeare reveals a deep understanding of nature's rhythms, its fragility, and its entanglement with human ambition, morality, and identity. Through rich imagery, dramatic symbolism, and poetic resonance, Shakespeare cultivates an environmental consciousness far ahead of his time.

Nature as Ethical and Political Terrain

In Shakespeare's tragedies especially, nature functions as a moral barometer. The natural world is responsive to human wrongdoing, and environmental disorder often mirrors political corruption. In Macbeth, for instance, the natural order collapses after Duncan's murder: day turns to night, noble falcons are slain by lowly owls, and horses devour each other. This upheaval signals that the crime committed is not only political but cosmic—a rupture of ecological as well as social balance.

Similarly, in King Lear, the storm that rages on the heath reflects the internal disarray of Lear's mind and the breakdown of filial and state order. Nature becomes both mirror and agent, participating in the moral drama of the play:

"The wrathful skies
Gallow the very wanderers of the dark,
And make them keep their caves."

Environmental thought here is interwoven with questions of justice, power, and disorder—anticipating modern ecological critiques of political systems that ignore environmental limits.

Pastoral and the Poetics of Place

Shakespeare's comedies and romances, by contrast, often locate environmental thought within the pastoral tradition. In plays like As You Like It and The Winter's Tale, the natural world offers refuge, clarity, and emotional rebirth. The Forest of Arden, in particular, serves as an ecological counterworld to the artificiality and corruption of the court:

"And this our life, exempt from public haunt,
Finds tongues in trees, books in the running brooks,
Sermons in stones, and good in everything."

These lines suggest a mode of environmental literacy—where nature is not just scenery, but a text to be read, a teacher to be heeded. Yet Shakespeare does not idealize the natural world uncritically. Even in pastoral settings, the environment is marked by labor, unpredictability, and a refusal to conform to human desires. Nature offers solace but demands respect; it heals, but it also humbles.

Ecological Interdependence and the Web of Life

Throughout his works, Shakespeare conveys a proto-ecological understanding of interdependence. The "Great Chain of Being," a Renaissance cosmology he often evokes, envisioned a hierarchical but interconnected system linking all forms of life—from earthworms to angels. When this chain is broken, the results are catastrophic.

In Hamlet, the image of rot spreading through Denmark uses natural decay to reflect political and moral corruption:

"Something is rotten in the state of Denmark."

This metaphor speaks to the interconnectedness of soil and state, of nature and nation. The language of disease and decay becomes ecological—an early recognition that when the foundations of the natural world are disrupted, human structures cannot remain intact.

Nature and the Limits of Control

The Tempest offers one of Shakespeare's most nuanced meditations on power, nature, and control. Prospero's ability to summon storms and command spirits like Ariel is symbolic of human efforts to master nature through knowledge. Yet the play ultimately questions the ethics of such mastery. The island itself resists full subjugation; its native inhabitant Caliban, though demonized, speaks passionately about his connection to the land:

"Be not afeard; the isle is full of noises,
Sounds and sweet airs, that give delight and hurt not."

Caliban's speech reminds us that environmental perception is not monopolized by those in power. His reverence for the land provides a counter-narrative to Prospero's dominion, suggesting an alternative way of being in nature—one based on coexistence rather than conquest.

Environmental Thought in the Sonnets

Shakespeare's environmental imagination is also evident in his sonnets. Sonnets 18 and 73, for example, dwell on the passage of seasons, the decay of the body, and the cycles of nature. In Sonnet 73:

"That time of year thou mayst in me behold
When yellow leaves, or none, or few, do hang..."

Here, nature becomes a metaphor for aging, but also a reflection on mortality's place in the ecological cycle. Shakespeare connects human emotion to the changing seasons, suggesting that environmental rhythms shape interior life just as much as external experience.

Conclusion: Toward an Early Environmental Ethics

Shakespeare did not write from an environmentalist perspective in the modern sense. However, his works display a profound awareness of the human relationship to the natural world—an awareness rooted in sensitivity, moral complexity, and poetic vision. From enchanted forests to storm-wracked heaths, from the decay of kingdoms to the beauty of springtime, Shakespeare shows us that nature is not separate from human life but intricately bound to it.

By revisiting Shakespeare's plays and poems through the lens of environmental thought, we gain not only a deeper appreciation of his artistry but also a richer vocabulary for addressing the ecological questions of our own time. His vision reminds us that the natural world is not a passive stage for human action, but a living, expressive force—one we ignore at our peril, and one we must continue to reimagine with care.

CHAPTER FIVE

Nature as Character and Force in Shakespeare's Drama

In the dramatic universe of William Shakespeare, nature is more than a scenic backdrop—it is a living presence, a force of consequence, and often, a character in its own right. Across tragedies, comedies, histories, and romances, Shakespeare imbues the natural world with agency and significance, allowing it to interact with human affairs as both an ally and adversary. His dramatization of nature anticipates modern ecological thinking by recognizing the natural world as responsive, moral, and deeply interconnected with human experience.

Nature as Moral Witness and Cosmic Judge

In many of Shakespeare's tragedies, nature functions as a moral force that reacts to human transgression. In

Macbeth, unnatural acts—particularly the murder of King Duncan—disrupt the natural order, and this disruption reverberates through the physical world:

"By th' clock 'tis day,
And yet dark night strangles the travelling lamp."
(Macbeth, 2.4)

This cosmic darkness is not mere atmosphere—it is the Earth itself recoiling from the crime. Similarly, in King Lear, the storm that erupts on the heath is more than a weather event; it mirrors Lear's inner chaos and the political betrayal that has unseated natural and familial order. Nature here acts as judge and chorus, amplifying the tragedy's emotional and ethical weight:

"Crack nature's molds, all germens spill at once
That make ingrateful man!"
(King Lear, 3.2)

The Storm as Speaking Force

Few natural elements in Shakespeare's plays are as vivid or emotionally charged as the storm. In The Tempest, the storm is intentionally conjured by Prospero's magic, serving not only as a dramatic device to shipwreck his enemies but also as a metaphor for upheaval and reckoning. While Prospero may direct the tempest, it is ultimately nature that holds power over the shipwrecked nobles, forcing humility and transformation.

In Julius Caesar, the night before Caesar's assassination is filled with unnatural phenomena: lions roaming the streets, slaves with burning hands, and men engulfed in flames. These omens from nature act as harbingers of political disaster and moral decay. Nature speaks in signs, demanding interpretation—a role not unlike that of a dramatic character whose actions drive the plot forward.

Forests and Wilderness: Nature as Space of Change

Nature's role as character is especially visible in Shakespeare's comedies and romances, where forests and wilderness often function as liminal zones—places of escape, disguise, transformation, and reconciliation. The Forest of Arden in As You Like It serves as a pastoral space in which social roles are dissolved and reconfigured:

"Are not these woods
More free from peril than the envious court?"
(As You Like It, 2.1)

In this space, nature becomes a character of restorative power. It does not merely set the scene for character development; it enables and catalyzes it. Similarly, the enchanted forest in A Midsummer Night's Dream transforms lovers and fools alike through its mischievous, magical ecology. The woods are alive—not just with fairies, but with the possibility of self-discovery.

Caliban and the Voice of the Earth

Nowhere is the fusion of character and nature more potent than in the figure of Caliban in The Tempest. As the son of the witch Sycorax and native of the island, Caliban embodies the land itself—uncultivated, defiant, and deeply rooted. Though often dehumanized by Prospero, Caliban's lyrical connection to the island gives him a voice of elemental poetry:

"The isle is full of noises,
Sounds and sweet airs, that give delight and hurt not."
(The Tempest, 3.2)

Caliban becomes a mouthpiece for nature, reminding us of the land's sensory richness and intrinsic value—beyond utility or conquest. His resistance to Prospero's domination symbolizes a deeper resistance of nature to total control.

Nature's Dual Role: Nurturing and Threatening

Shakespeare's natural world is never one-dimensional. It can nurture and heal, as in the restorative scenes in The Winter's Tale or the romantic forests of Twelfth Night, but it can also destroy. The sea in Pericles and The Tempest separates families, swallows ships, and tests human endurance. Nature is both maternal and monstrous, beautiful and brutal—its ambivalence is what gives it such dramatic power.

Conclusion: A Dramatic Ecology

Shakespeare's dramatization of nature as a character and force reveals a sophisticated ecological imagination. By giving nature voice, agency, and moral dimension, he challenges the anthropocentric worldview of his time and ours. His plays remind us that the Earth is not passive—it responds, it remembers, and it transforms. In elevating nature from setting to co-actor, Shakespeare laid the groundwork for an environmental vision that continues to resonate in an age of ecological crisis.

CHAPTER SIX

Between Tempest and Tranquility: Nature's Duality in Shakespeare

In the works of William Shakespeare, nature is not merely a passive backdrop to human affairs but an active and often ambivalent presence. It manifests as storm and sunlight, chaos and harmony, threat and sanctuary. From the violent gales of King Lear to the peace of the Forest of Arden, Shakespeare repeatedly explores the dual nature of the environment—its power to unsettle as well as to heal. This dynamic vision captures nature's paradoxical role in human life: it is both tempest and tranquility, destruction and refuge.

The Tempest as a Symbol of Nature's Fury

Perhaps the most emblematic example of nature's destructive power appears in The Tempest, where a shipwreck begins the narrative. The titular storm—conjured by Prospero's magic—reflects both human will and nature's uncontainable violence:

"Blow, till thou burst thy wind, if room enough!"
(The Tempest, 1.1)

The tempest, though orchestrated, embodies elemental force. It disrupts social order, flings characters across an enchanted island, and initiates a transformative journey. Yet even as it evokes fear and danger, the storm becomes a necessary rupture—forcing characters into self-confrontation and eventual reconciliation. Nature's fury, then, is not arbitrary—it is purposeful, pushing toward moral and emotional regeneration.

King Lear: The Storm Within and Without

In King Lear, the tempest is not magical but existential. As Lear rages on the heath, exposed to wind and rain, the storm externalizes his psychological collapse and political ruin:

"Blow, winds, and crack your cheeks! Rage! Blow!"
(King Lear, 3.2)

The storm here is both metaphor and mirror, reflecting Lear's inner turmoil and the unnaturalness of familial betrayal. Nature becomes a stage for emotional truth, its violence echoing the social disintegration of the play. But even amid the storm, there are moments of clarity and compassion—especially in Lear's newfound empathy for the "poor naked wretches" of his kingdom. Thus, the tempest is not solely a force of destruction, but also of revelation.

The Forest of Arden and Natural Refuge

In contrast to the destructive energies of storm and sea, Shakespeare often depicts nature as a refuge of tranquility and renewal. Nowhere is this more evident than in the Forest of Arden in As You Like It. Here, exiles from court find not only safety but philosophical insight and emotional healing:

"Here feel we but the penalty of Adam,
The seasons' difference; as the icy fang
And churlish chiding of the winter's wind..."
(As You Like It, 2.1)

Nature's trials are acknowledged, but they are also seen as honest and egalitarian—free from the corruption and deceit of courtly life. The forest offers characters the space to reflect, disguise, reconcile, and grow. It is tranquil not because it is tame, but because it allows for natural, unforced transformation.

Nature in the Sonnets: Cycles of Decay and Renewal

Shakespeare's sonnets, too, explore nature's duality, especially in relation to time, beauty, and mortality. Sonnet 18 celebrates nature's gentle beauty, while also acknowledging its impermanence:

"Rough winds do shake the darling buds of May,
And summer's lease hath all too short a date."

This gentle turbulence is a reminder of nature's temporal rhythm—a balance of bloom and blight. In Sonnet 73, nature's fading colors in autumn symbolize the aging poet's waning vitality, but even here, there is dignity and peace in accepting the cycle:

"Bare ruined choirs, where late the sweet birds sang..."

Nature offers both melancholy and comfort—a graceful reminder of life's impermanence and continuity.

The Island in The Tempest: From Chaos to Calm

By the end of The Tempest, the same island that begins as a site of shipwreck and confusion becomes a place of healing and resolution. The wildness of the natural world is not eradicated but integrated. Prospero, who once sought to dominate nature, ultimately renounces his magic and prepares to re-enter society:

"I'll break my staff... I'll drown my book."

This gesture signals a shift from control to harmony. The island's elemental forces—wind, wave, forest, and spirit—have accomplished their work. Nature's dual aspects converge in this moment: it has been both tempest and tranquility, trial and teacher.

Conclusion: Shakespeare's Ecological Imagination

Shakespeare's portrayal of nature's duality speaks to a profound ecological imagination. His works recognize that the natural world is not monolithic—it can destroy, but it also nourishes; it can isolate, but it also connects. Nature in Shakespeare is a force of transformation, neither wholly benign nor entirely hostile.

In an age increasingly defined by environmental crisis, Shakespeare's vision remains urgent. His dramas remind us that the Earth is a partner in the human story—not a silent backdrop, but a speaking, shifting presence. Between tempest and tranquility, we are called to listen, to learn, and to live with nature rather than above it.

CHAPTER SEVEN

Human Nature and Nonhuman Agency in the Shakespearean Imagination

In the Shakespearean imagination, the boundary between the human and the nonhuman is far from rigid. Whether in the whispering forests of A Midsummer Night's Dream, the storm-lashed heath of King Lear, or the enchanted island of The Tempest, Shakespeare infuses the natural world with agency, presence, and even personality. He suggests that human nature is inextricably entangled with nonhuman forces—weather, animals, spirits, and landscapes—that act not merely as background but as participants in the dramatic unfolding of human lives. This deep interconnection anticipates contemporary ecological thought, particularly theories of nonhuman agency, which argue that the environment and other nonhuman entities possess forms of power and influence independent of human control.

The Natural World as Actor and Agent

In plays such as The Tempest, Shakespeare goes beyond the metaphorical to stage nature as a direct agent. The storm that opens the play is a tangible force that drives the plot, separating characters and initiating the process of reckoning and redemption. Though conjured by Prospero's magic, the tempest has its own volatile energy—unpredictable, uncontrollable, and transformative:

"What care these roarers for the name of king?"
(The Tempest, 1.1)

This line not only dismisses human authority in the face of natural power but frames nature as indifferent to political hierarchy, underscoring its autonomy. The sea, the wind, and the spirits of the island are not passive tools—they reshape human experience and reveal deeper truths.

Trees That Speak and Animals That Symbolize

Throughout Shakespeare's canon, animals and natural phenomena are used to reflect and refract human emotions, but they also exist with their own symbolic and narrative integrity. The raven in Macbeth, the lion in A Midsummer Night's Dream, the weather in King Lear, and the sea across many plays are granted affective and interpretive power.

In King Lear, nature is not merely symbolic but acts upon characters. The storm does not only mirror Lear's inner turmoil—it drives him toward madness, humility, and insight. Nonhuman agency is not just background noise; it is instrumental to human transformation.

"You owe me no subscription: then let fall
Your horrible pleasure..."
(King Lear, 3.2)

Lear speaks to the storm as if it were a sentient being—an adversary with intention. This dramatization of interaction between human and nonhuman reflects an early recognition of agency beyond the human.

Caliban and the Voice of the Nonhuman

Caliban, in The Tempest, stands as a complex figure of nonhuman agency. While technically human, Caliban is deeply associated with the earth, the wild, and the elemental. His language and behavior mark him as part of the island's ecology rather than the world of civilization and artifice. Through Caliban, Shakespeare voices the land's memory, resistance, and vitality:

"This island's mine, by Sycorax my mother..."
(The Tempest, 1.2)

Caliban's deep bond with the island positions him as an expression of the nonhuman world's will—a representative of the landscape's agency against colonial domination. His articulation of the island's "noises" and "sweet airs" brings the island's sensory life into the center of the play, elevating the environment from background to subject.

Nonhuman Spirits and Material Intelligence

In A Midsummer Night's Dream, the woods teem with spirits, fairies, and natural magic. Puck, Oberon, and Titania manipulate not only human perception but also the seasons and weather. The play's forest is not just a setting for mischief; it is a living force, altering behavior, disrupting social order, and facilitating transformation.

Nature here is theatrical—filled with agency, mobility, and unpredictability. Human characters are constantly subject to the whims of the natural world, which becomes both mirror and maker of change. This animistic rendering suggests that agency is distributed across species and spaces.

Beyond Metaphor: Shakespeare's Proto-Ecological Vision

While it is tempting to read Shakespeare's nature as purely metaphorical—symbolizing inner states or moral ideas—his works often resist such reduction. Instead, they propose a dynamic ontology in which human and nonhuman lives are woven together. The environment shapes destiny, spirit creatures intervene in human affairs, and the material world—rocks, seas, forests—demands ethical attention.

This view aligns with current posthumanist and ecological critiques that challenge the human/nonhuman divide and reimagine agency as dispersed across a more-than-human world. Shakespeare does not simply represent nature—he listens to it, stages it, and imagines its power to act.

Conclusion: A Drama of Entanglement

Shakespeare's plays are dramas of entanglement, where the actions of kings are disrupted by storms, where forests whisper transformations, and where animals, spirits, and landscapes participate in the moral and emotional fabric of human life. His imagination recognizes that human nature cannot be understood apart from the nonhuman forces that shape, confront, and coexist with it.

By attributing agency to the nonhuman world, Shakespeare opens a space for ecological awareness—one that urges us to recognize our embeddedness within a larger web of life. In doing so, he anticipates a critical shift in environmental thought: that the Earth is not a silent stage for human drama, but a voice, a force, and a character in its own right.

CHAPTER EIGHT

READING SHAKESPEARE IN THE AGE OF CLIMATE CRISIS

In an age defined by melting ice caps, rising seas, and burning forests, the relevance of classical literature might seem distant. Yet, William Shakespeare's plays, written over four centuries ago, offer surprising insight into humanity's relationship with the natural world. By re-reading Shakespeare through an ecocritical lens, we uncover urgent reflections on ecological balance, environmental ethics, and the consequences of human hubris—concerns that resonate powerfully in our time of climate crisis.

Nature as Character and Force

Shakespeare did not treat nature as mere backdrop. In many of his plays, nature functions almost as a character—an active force influencing human fate. In King Lear, the storm on the heath mirrors Lear's psychological collapse, but it also serves as a violent reminder of nature's indifference to human authority. Stripped of his power, Lear confronts the raw power of the elements: "Blow, winds, and crack your cheeks! rage! blow!" This moment strips away the illusion of dominion over nature, a theme acutely relevant as modern societies grapple with environmental disasters of their own making.

Similarly, in The Tempest, the island is more than a setting; it is a dynamic space shaped by and responsive to human presence. Prospero's control over the elements—through his magic—raises questions about power, colonization, and ecological manipulation. As contemporary societies seek to engineer climate solutions, Shakespeare's magical island invites reflection on the ethical boundaries of environmental intervention.

The Forest as Refuge and Critique

In comedies like As You Like It and A Midsummer Night's Dream, forests serve as spaces of transformation and resistance to the corruption of court or city life. The Forest of Arden, in particular, offers a vision of pastoral simplicity and ecological harmony. Duke Senior, exiled from court, reflects, "And this our life, exempt from public haunt, / Finds tongues in trees, books in the running brooks." This vision romanticizes nature, but it also critiques the social and political order by proposing an alternative rooted in simplicity and interdependence.

Yet Shakespeare's nature is never one-dimensional. In A Midsummer Night's Dream, the feud between Titania and Oberon disrupts the seasons, causing "contagious fogs," "hoary-headed frosts," and failed harvests—an ecological imbalance caused by supernatural conflict. Though fantastical, this disruption anticipates modern concerns over climate destabilization caused by human conflict and industrial excess.

Shakespeare and Ecocriticism

Ecocriticism—the study of literature's relationship with the environment—has illuminated how deeply Shakespeare engages with ecological thought. Far from being environmentally neutral, his works grapple with questions of sustainability, stewardship, and disruption. In an era when the natural world is undergoing dramatic transformation, Shakespeare's plays remind us of nature's power, fragility, and autonomy.

Moreover, his works offer models of ecological awareness. While not an environmentalist in the modern sense, Shakespeare presents nature as something with agency—often beautiful, sometimes brutal, and always beyond full human control. This perspective is invaluable today, as climate activists urge a move away from extractive, anthropocentric thinking toward a more respectful and reciprocal relationship with the Earth.

Conclusion: The Bard and the Planet

Reading Shakespeare in the age of climate crisis is not an exercise in anachronism—it is a recognition of literature's power to shape how we think about the world. His plays reflect a worldview in which nature is integral to human experience, both materially and morally. As we face ecological catastrophe, Shakespeare's enduring insights invite us to reconsider not only how we live in the world, but also how we imagine our place within it.

CHAPTER NINE

GREEN SHAKESPEARE: SUSTAINABILITY AND THE STAGE

Past and Present

In recent years, environmental sustainability has moved from the margins to the mainstream of cultural discourse. Amid global calls to address climate change, pollution, and resource depletion, artists and institutions are reevaluating their role in promoting ecological consciousness. One surprising yet fertile area of exploration lies in the works of William Shakespeare. Though he lived in the Elizabethan era, Shakespeare's plays reveal a deep sensitivity to the natural world—a sensitivity that modern theatre-makers are now embracing through both thematic reinterpretation and sustainable production practices.

Shakespeare's works are filled with forests, storms, gardens, and wild landscapes that play more than just symbolic roles—they influence character, plot, and meaning. In As You Like It, the Forest of Arden is a transformative space, offering refuge from courtly corruption and a place for personal renewal. Duke Senior's lines, "And this our life, exempt from public haunt, / Finds tongues in trees, books in the running brooks," speak to a profound respect for nature as a teacher and healer.

In The Tempest, the island setting is nearly sentient, its magic and mystery rooted in elemental forces. Prospero's control over the island's weather and terrain represents both human ambition and the dangers of manipulating the natural order. These works provide a lens through which modern audiences can reflect on contemporary environmental challenges.

The recognition of Shakespeare's ecological vision has inspired a wave of sustainable theatrical practices around the world. Theatre companies are not only staging Shakespeare's plays with environmental themes in mind—they are also transforming how those productions are created.

The Royal Shakespeare Company (RSC) in the UK has taken significant steps toward reducing its environmental impact. This includes cutting paper use, reusing costumes and sets, and adopting energy-efficient lighting. The RSC's recent strategic plan outlines goals to reduce carbon emissions and promote sustainable touring practices. Productions such as As You Like It have been reimagined with minimalistic, nature-based sets to emphasize ecological themes.

Shakespeare's Globe in London has also adopted sustainability as a core value. Beyond the plays themselves, the organization focuses on responsible sourcing of materials, recycling, and reducing travel footprints. In 2021, the Globe launched a sustainability policy that includes eco-conscious design principles for their in-house products and programs. Educational initiatives like "Sustainable Shakespeare" link performance with broader environmental learning, ensuring that ecological awareness reaches both audiences and students.

In the United States, the Island Shakespeare Festival in Washington state is committed to becoming a zero-waste operation by 2025. Their open-air productions and community outreach programs are designed to be as low-impact as possible, blending theatre with environmental activism.

Educational Impact and Future Directions

One of the most exciting developments in Green Shakespeare has been the rise of education-based initiatives that merge performance with environmental engagement. The Green Shakespeare project in Milan and Stratford-upon-Avon has pioneered outdoor adaptations of Shakespeare's works in botanical gardens, encouraging audiences to view both the plays and the planet with fresh eyes. Performances like A Walk in Shakespeare's Garden connect the beauty of the Bard's language with the biodiversity of real-world environments.

The Shakespeare Birthplace Trust has also joined the movement with events promoting ecological awareness at the playwright's family homes. Their "Big Green Month" event highlights sustainability through exhibitions, lectures, and interactive garden experiences.

These efforts reflect a broader trend: recognizing the power of classical literature to inspire contemporary action. As the climate crisis escalates, Shakespeare's works provide not only cultural continuity but also ethical inquiry. His reverence for the natural world—and his cautionary portrayals of its exploitation—can inform a new generation of artists, educators, and audiences.

Conclusion

Green Shakespeare is more than an academic lens; it is a practical and philosophical approach to art-making in the 21st century. By engaging with sustainability both on the stage and behind the scenes, theatres around the world are reshaping the legacy of the world's most famous playwright. As climate challenges intensify, the theatre's embrace of ecological responsibility offers a powerful model for how storytelling can lead to stewardship.

CHAPTER TEN

Elizabethan Echoes in Today's Environmental Discourse

As the world grapples with escalating climate crises, historians, scholars, and literary critics have increasingly turned to the past to unearth ecological wisdom embedded in cultural traditions. The Elizabethan era, marked by the reign of Queen Elizabeth I (1558–1603), is one such period where early environmental awareness—though not articulated in the terms we use today—can be discerned in literature, policy, and popular belief. Surprisingly, this era echoes loudly in today's environmental discourse, offering insights into how human societies have long negotiated their relationship with the natural world.

From the philosophical underpinnings of natural order in Renaissance thought to Shakespearean portrayals of weather, land, and the cosmos, the Elizabethan worldview provides a mirror through which modern ecological anxieties can be better understood. Far from being irrelevant, the ecological imagination of the Elizabethans challenges us to rethink our assumptions about progress, nature, and sustainability.

The Natural Order and Human Responsibility

The Elizabethans inherited a worldview shaped by the "Great Chain of Being"—a hierarchical structure believed to organize all matter and life. God stood at the top, followed by angels, humans, animals, plants, and minerals. This cosmic order emphasized harmony and interdependence. To disrupt this order, especially through acts of greed or hubris, was to invite chaos.

Today's ecological crises—from deforestation and biodiversity loss to climate change—can be viewed through a similar lens. Just as Elizabethans feared that upsetting the natural order would have dire consequences, modern environmentalists argue that unchecked exploitation of the earth's resources will inevitably lead to collapse. The parallel is striking: both paradigms warn of the dangers of overstepping natural bounds.

Moreover, the Elizabethans valued stewardship, particularly in rural communities dependent on agriculture. Concepts akin to "sustainability" existed, if not by name then by practice. Land management had to consider long-term fertility, and common lands were vital for collective well-being. In modern environmentalism, these ideas find expression in regenerative agriculture and communal land trusts—practices that reflect enduring concerns about shared responsibility for natural resources.

Shakespeare's Environmental Vision

Perhaps the most powerful Elizabethan voice still heard today is that of William Shakespeare. His plays are rich with environmental imagery, metaphors of weather and wilderness, and explorations of human interaction with the non-human world. These texts not only reflect ecological concerns of his time—such as the Little Ice Age and changing land use—but also offer timeless insights into how we experience nature.

In King Lear, the storm on the heath is more than weather—it is a symbolic eruption of disorder in both the kingdom and the natural world. Lear's descent into madness mirrors environmental chaos, illustrating how societal breakdown often parallels ecological unraveling. Similarly, The Tempest positions nature as a force of retribution and renewal. Prospero's island is both paradise and prison, shaped by human ambition and magical control. These portrayals resonate with today's climate-induced disasters, which force us to confront the consequences of manipulating ecosystems for human ends.

Shakespeare's forests, such as the Forest of Arden in As You Like It, present a different model: one of refuge and restoration. Here, nature provides space for reflection, healing, and moral clarity. In contemporary environmental discourse, this aligns with the concept of biophilia—the innate human need to connect with the natural world for psychological and spiritual well-being.

The Material Culture of the Elizabethans

Environmental consciousness can also be seen in the Elizabethan material world. The use of local materials in building, the reliance on seasonal foods, and the limitations on waste were not necessarily ideological but practical. Yet these practices fostered a form of ecological balance that today's zero-waste movements and locavore food systems strive to emulate.

Even Elizabethan theatre reflected a sensitivity to ecological limits. The open-air Globe Theatre, for instance, relied on natural light, minimal props, and reused costumes. This frugality was born of necessity but resonates with today's efforts to create sustainable art spaces and performances. "Green theatre" today—where productions minimize carbon footprints and promote ecological themes—can find an unlikely precedent in the resourceful ingenuity of Elizabethan stagecraft.

Nature and Superstition: Spiritual Ecology

Elizabethan England also possessed a spiritual ecology that blended folklore, superstition, and proto-scientific thought. Natural elements were believed to have agency: storms were signs of divine displeasure, comets foretold disaster, and forests were imbued with mystery. While much of this has been dismissed as superstition, it reveals a worldview in which nature was not inert or exploitable but alive with meaning.

This perspective shares surprising affinities with certain strains of modern environmentalism, particularly Indigenous ecological knowledge and the Gaia hypothesis, which regard the Earth as a living organism. As science increasingly acknowledges the intelligence of plants, the communicative capacity of animals, and the self-regulating systems of ecosystems, the Elizabethan belief in an animate world appears less naïve and more visionary.

In A Midsummer Night's Dream, for instance, the disruption of the fairy world causes environmental chaos—crops fail, seasons shift, and diseases spread. Titania's lament about "hoary-headed frosts / Fall in the fresh lap of the crimson rose" is a poetic rendering of ecological imbalance. Today, this mirrors climate science's warnings about how small disturbances can have cascading planetary effects.

Echoes in Policy and Ethics

The Elizabethan period also offers early glimpses of environmental regulation. Laws on land use, forest conservation, and water rights were rudimentary but present. The enclosure movement—privatizing common lands—sparked social unrest and debates about access to nature that remain relevant today, particularly in discussions around environmental justice and the right to a healthy environment.

Furthermore, Elizabethan ethical thinking, influenced by classical texts and Christian doctrine, often emphasized moderation and humility—virtues sorely needed in a consumer-driven modern world. The ideal of temperance, of living within limits, is echoed in the contemporary call for degrowth and sustainable living.

Elizabethan thinkers such as Francis Bacon also laid the groundwork for the scientific revolution, promoting empirical inquiry and the mastery of nature. While Bacon's legacy is complex—often criticized for enabling extractive science—his emphasis on understanding the natural world as a source of knowledge, not just exploitation, remains influential. Today's environmental science continues this legacy, though increasingly tempered by a recognition of nature's limits.

Conclusion: Rethinking Progress Through the Past

To read the Elizabethan era as an ecological text is not to romanticize the past or ignore its contradictions. The same period saw colonial expansion, the exploitation of natural resources, and the early stirrings of industrial capitalism. Yet within its literature, philosophy, and everyday life are fragments of an environmental ethic that speaks powerfully to our own time.

The Elizabethans lived with a visceral awareness of the land, the seasons, and the fragility of life. They feared famine, revered the forests, and read the skies for meaning. These habits of thought and imagination, though shaped by a different world, offer tools for reimagining our own relationship with the Earth.

In reconnecting with the ecological insights of the Elizabethan world, we might find not only historical perspective but also the seeds of a more sustainable future. The echoes are there—we need only to listen.

CHAPTER ELEVEN

THE BARD AND THE BIOSPHERE: ECOLOGICAL LESSONS

Shakespeare in the Anthropocene

In the Anthropocene—a geological epoch defined by humanity's dominant impact on the Earth—literature offers not just historical insight but also philosophical grounding for ecological reflection. Among the many voices that echo across time, William Shakespeare stands out. Although he wrote centuries before the rise of modern environmentalism, Shakespeare's works contain a remarkable awareness of nature's agency, human dependence on ecological balance, and the ethical consequences of environmental disruption.

In an age increasingly defined by climate crises, biodiversity loss, and ecological collapse, revisiting the works of Shakespeare allows us to engage with the natural world through a cultural and moral lens. His plays reflect the complexities of environmental relationships long before "ecology" became a scientific term. By tracing nature's role in his drama—whether as setting, symbol, or active force—we uncover a rich archive of ecological wisdom that remains profoundly relevant.

Shakespeare's Environmental Imagination

Nature in Shakespeare's plays is not a mere backdrop; it is a dynamic presence that shapes character, mood, and moral order. Forests, storms, rivers, islands, and gardens are not inert spaces but active agents that facilitate transformation, challenge human authority, and mirror social or psychological states.

In King Lear, the wild heath becomes a theatre of both madness and revelation. Lear, stripped of his power and cast into the storm, experiences the fury of nature not only as external chaos but also as an inward reckoning. The storm reflects the collapse of political and familial structures while forcing Lear to confront his own human fragility. His words—"I am a man more sinned against than sinning"—underscore an ecological humility that resonates with today's environmental discourse: the recognition that human arrogance invites natural retribution.

Similarly, in The Tempest, Prospero's control of the island is symbolic of colonial and ecological dominance. Yet the natural world, through the spirits Ariel and Caliban, resists and responds. Prospero's eventual renunciation of magic can be interpreted as a gesture toward ecological reconciliation—a relinquishing of mastery over nature in favor of coexistence and respect.

Land, Labor, and Resource Use in the Plays

Shakespeare's England was a land in transition. The early modern period saw dramatic shifts in land use, from feudal agrarian systems to enclosure and proto-capitalist privatization. These transformations brought both economic opportunity and environmental exploitation. Shakespeare was attuned to these tensions, and his plays often reflect anxiety about the commodification of nature.

In Richard II, the metaphor of England as a "precious stone set in the silver sea" gives way to lament over "this England that was wont to conquer others / Hath made a shameful conquest of itself." Here, the selling off of land and resources is linked to moral decline and national crisis. This early critique of environmental degradation through political mismanagement echoes contemporary concerns about the extractive logic that drives climate change and resource depletion.

As You Like It presents an alternative view: a pastoral retreat into the Forest of Arden, where characters reflect on simplicity, nature, and the flaws of courtly life. While not free of idealization, the forest functions as a space of renewal, dialogue, and ethical insight—much like the modern environmental movement's celebration of wilderness as a site for reflection and resistance.

The Weather as Moral and Ecological Force

Weather in Shakespeare is rarely neutral. It is often charged with moral significance and narrative weight. Storms, droughts, and strange seasons are signs of imbalance—both in the natural world and the human realm. These "eco-symbols" prefigure the climate discourse of our own age.

In Macbeth, the eerie weather that follows Duncan's murder—"unnatural deeds / Do breed unnatural troubles"—speaks to the disruption of the natural order. Nature revolts at human violence, suggesting a deep interconnection between ethical and ecological balance.

In A Midsummer Night's Dream, Titania describes how the conflict among the fairies has wrought environmental chaos: "The seasons alter: hoary-headed frosts / Fall in the fresh lap of the crimson rose." This fusion of myth and meteorology anticipates modern ecological thinking, which understands that social conflict, political disruption, and environmental change are interdependent systems.

The use of weather as a narrative force in Shakespeare's plays reflects a belief that the natural world responds to human behavior—a theme that aligns with current understandings of feedback loops in climate systems and the concept of planetary boundaries.

Non-Human Agency and Environmental Ethics

Another important ecological lesson from Shakespeare is his treatment of non-human agency. Animals, trees, rivers, and spirits are given voice, intention, and moral relevance. This breaks with purely mechanistic views of nature and encourages a more inclusive ethical framework.

Caliban in The Tempest is often interpreted as a figure of colonized humanity, but he also represents an indigenous connection to the land. His speech—"Be not afeard; the isle is full of noises"—reveals a sensory, emotional, and spiritual bond with nature that contrasts with Prospero's extractive relationship. Caliban's knowledge of the island is experiential and reciprocal, not dominative.

In Coriolanus, the plebeians' hunger and struggle for grain highlight the centrality of food systems, agriculture, and environmental justice. The distribution of natural resources is a question not just of economy but of ethics. This mirrors modern concerns about food security, water rights, and the unequal impacts of climate change on vulnerable populations.

By foregrounding the experiences of non-dominant voices—whether human or non-human—Shakespeare cultivates a perspective of ecological empathy, inviting audiences to expand their moral horizons beyond the self and the species.

The Garden as Ecological Allegory

Gardens are recurring symbols in Shakespeare's plays, often serving as allegories for political and ecological order. In Richard II, the gardener compares the state to a neglected garden: "Our sea-walled garden, the whole land / Is full of weeds, her fairest flowers chok'd up." The metaphor captures the link between governance and environmental care.

Gardens in Shakespeare are not simply places of leisure—they are sites of labor, control, and cultivation. Yet they also reveal the limits of human power. Nature grows wild, resists pruning, and challenges artificial order. This duality mirrors today's tension between conservation and rewilding, management and spontaneity, control and surrender.

The Elizabethan garden was a space of design and dominance, but also of biodiversity and reflection. Shakespeare uses the garden to suggest that human culture must coexist with nature's autonomy—not override it.

Shakespeare in the Environmental Humanities

In recent years, Shakespeare has become a central figure in the field of environmental humanities. Scholars and theatre practitioners alike have explored how his works can serve as texts for ecological education, activism, and sustainability.

"Green Shakespeare" productions are increasingly common, with theatre companies staging plays in outdoor settings, using recycled materials, and thematizing environmental issues. For example, some modern productions of The Tempest portray the island as a climate-ravaged landscape, casting Prospero as a scientist or industrialist and Caliban as an ecological martyr.

Academic initiatives have also flourished. Programs like "Shakespeare and Ecology" investigate how early modern texts can inform current debates on environmental ethics, resilience, and the Anthropocene. These interdisciplinary efforts bridge literature, ecology, philosophy, and performance, demonstrating the enduring relevance of the Bard's ecological insights.

Conclusion: A Shakespearean Ecology of Mind

Shakespeare's works teach us to listen to the land, to respect the limits of power, and to recognize the intricate entanglement of human and non-human worlds. His plays reflect an ecological consciousness that, while shaped by Renaissance cosmology, speaks urgently to our present planetary predicament.

The biosphere—our shared, fragile life-support system—is not unlike Shakespeare's stage: filled with drama, tension, interconnection, and moral consequence. By engaging with the Bard through an ecological lens, we do not merely find historical curiosities but timeless truths about living within limits, honoring the Earth, and understanding that every action reverberates through a web of life.

In an era of ecological reckoning, Shakespeare reminds us of the need for humility, imagination, and moral clarity. His vision, layered with complexity and care, helps us see not only who we are but how we might live better with the world around us.

References

Garrard, Greg. Ecocriticism. 2nd ed., Routledge, 2012.

Estok, Simon C. Ecocriticism and Shakespeare: Reading Ecophobia. Palgrave Macmillan, 2011.

Bruckner, Lynne, and Dan Brayton, editors. Ecocritical Shakespeare. Ashgate, 2011.

Hall, Kim F. "Guess Who's Coming to Dinner? Colonization and Miscegenation in The Tempest." Adaptations of Shakespeare: An Anthology of Plays from the 17th Century to the Present, edited by Daniel Fischlin and Mark Fortier, Routledge, 2000, pp. 121–140.

Mentz, Steve. Ocean. Bloomsbury Academic, 2020.

Roberts, Gareth. "The Eco-conscious Shakespeare." Green Letters: Studies in Ecocriticism, vol. 11, no. 1, 2010, pp. 10–21. Taylor & Francis Online, https://doi.org/10.1080/14688417.2010.10590077

Westling, Louise. "Shakespeare and the Anthropocene." The Cambridge Companion to Literature and the Environment, edited by Louise Westling, Cambridge UP, 2014, pp. 67–80.

Berry, Philippa. Shakespeare's Feminine Endings: Disfiguring Death in the Tragedies. Routledge, 1999.

Neill, Michael. "Broken English and Green Worlds: Language and Ecology in Shakespeare." Shakespeare and the Natural World, edited by Tom MacFaul, Cambridge UP, 2015, pp. 102–117.

Munroe, Jennifer. Ecological Approaches to Early Modern English Texts: A Field Guide to Reading. Ashgate, 2015.